Another Tanners Worth

Another Tanners Worth

MAUREEN MASON

authorHOUSE®

AuthorHouse™
1663 Liberty Drive
Bloomington, IN 47403
www.authorhouse.com
Phone: 1-800-839-8640

Published by AuthorHouse   07/13/2012

ISBN: 978-1-4772-1370-4 (sc)
ISBN: 978-1-4772-1371-1 (e)

Table of Contents

When I published my first book in 2008

'Sixpence in my Shoe'
I had no thoughts about writing another one, yet here I am four years
down the road with my second one.

'Another Tanners Worth'
I do hope that those of you who bought my first book enjoyed the
read enough to join me on this second journey into poetry, and to the
new reader I hope that you enjoy the experience

Maureen Mason

This Precious Gift

On this special day I give to you
A gift that comes from my heart
You cannot touch, or hold it
But with this you'll never part
Within this special package
Is all the love I hold for you
For today, and tomorrow,
our whole lives through
Until we meet again
There are a host of precious memories
That I'm passing on to you
From the time we met and fell in love
To the day I married you
Then to follow, more precious yet
The time when our children were born
The light in your eyes, the look on your face
When you introduced me to each one
All these treasures are wrapped in gold
'Tis the light of my love for you
Take this gift and treasure it
Until the time when we must part
Hold it close and keep it safe
Just lock it in your heart.

My Story

Four hundred words are not enough
For all that I want to say
About the slums where we grew up
And the old mill where we used to play.

Our very first holiday to Mablethorpe
Where we stayed in a caravan
Evacuation is what we were told
At the station by the man

Or when we came back to Armley
And the night of the big air raid
When a soldier ran off with our baby brother
An event that really scared my Mother

The bonfire we had at the end of the war
And the model of the Guy that we made
Mushy peas, pork pies and toffee apples
They were all home made.

There never was much brass to spend
Though we worked for every penny
At least twelve hours every day
Dahn't pit or on't Spinning Jenny

The schoolyard games we used to play
Were always the same, day after day,
It was whip and top, hopscotch and skipping.
And then for tea; lots of bread and jam,
Treacle or dripping.

Five-minute fiction might be the name
And I have done my best.
Those four hundred words are not enough
And don't touch the tip of the rest

Poetry

Poetry is beauty, rhythm and grace,
The beauty of a smile on a little one's face
In the waves that travel across the seas
And the breeze that rustles through the trees

There is poetry in the horrors of war
Those majestic heroes gone before
In the misery and pain of the utmost grief
And when peace comes at last, it's beyond belief

It is the ability to express how we feel
To make our wildest dreams become real
Also known as the breath of life,
The love that grows between a man and his wife

Poetry is known as the music of life,
in the rhythms and melodies
that soothe away strife
Expressed in the beauty of a dance
Bringing joy to the world with every chance

This is such a wonderful art composing words
that that come from the heart
It appreciates beauty and wisdom and love
All these are special gifts sent from above

What Is Love?

What is this thing called love 'twixt you and I
An emotion that will be ours until we die?
For me it was the very first time I saw your face
Heard your voice and saw you smile.

It is the look in your eyes each time we meet
And the touch of your hand on mine.
The way your face lit up each moment
that we spent together,
Like sunshine after a thunderstorm
and the lightening of the weather.

It is the day that you proposed
to spend your whole life with me,
And the sound of the birdsong at dawn
This vast choir in the tree.

It is in the magic of our baby's very first cry,
This beautiful child that is born to you and I
The pain we feel when at last we have to part
Each knowing that the other holds your heart

It is the pain and suffering of that parting breath.
When those beloved eyelids close in death
We will remember when at last we meet again
In Heaven together on God's highest Plain

An Angel

Angels are ethereal beings
They usually have enormous wings
But if they ever visit earth
They're just like other human beings

If you ever meet an angel
You wouldn't know it right away
The halo and the wings are left in heaven
To wear on another day

I was lucky to have met an angel
Just the other day, she must
have known I needed company
and walked beside me all the way

We walked we shopped we chatted
Had fun the whole day long
And never have I regretted
The day she came along

I knew she was an Angel
She was always there for me
If ever I was down or glum
I knew that I could turn to her
Because she was my Mum!!

Message for Today's Youth

Go out and search your farthest horizons
Aim high for those precious goals.
Hold a kind thought for your friends, and neighbours,
Then you'll be at peace with your soul.

Don't ever lose your capacity for caring,
It has grown with you since you were a child.
There's a world full of wonders for you to discover.
Just reach out, and live life to the full.

The years of your life will change as the seasons,
You have just reached the springtime of youth,
I urge you, go out and live each single moment
Finding peace, wisdom and truth

Live your life to the full,
and when your wintertime comes
You will have memories to treasure
and no time for regrets.

My Four Boys

Around my neck encased in gold
They are always close to my heart
Of course they are only pictures
From which I shall never part.

The first one is about twenty three
He is the man that I married
The next is my first grandchild
The only one my eldest ever carried

The third one is just a year younger
And born to my youngest lass
Now he has reached twenty two
Oh dear! how the years fly past

The fourth one is the youngest one
He's just turned fifteen
A set of lads more handsome
Have never yet been seen

When the youngest boy was just a babe
He used to climb upon my knee
I'd like to look at Grandmas boys
If you have time to show them to me

Fortieth Birthday

I send you all my love today
And hope when you read this,
You'll think of me across the sea
Knowing that I'm with you.

I hope the gift I chose for you
will make you smile today,
And that you won't be too, too sad,
if the lines don't go away.

So have your face lift, body wrap,
massage or what you will
Just always know my darling girl
I love you and always will

Fairies

We have little people in our garden
Flower Fairies, that's who they are,
They come to us every morning
And sleep every night on a star

We don't know where they have come from
Although we do know what they do
They take care of the flowers in our gardens
For folks like me and you

They fly in the skies and sleep on the clouds
When wintertime comes along
And help Santa Claus to load up his sleigh
It will be Christmas before very long

This year however it's different
And no one can understand why
But this year carnations are blooming
Under a cold November sky

It must be a part of the magic
That we were brought up to believe
I wonder what other mysteries
They are hiding under their sleeve?

Maybe there will be snowdrops
Under a cool harvest moon
Or are they just trying to tell us
Global warming is coming too soon

Paradise

Have you ever thought about Paradise?
What is paradise?
Have you ever been there?
That is a thought to conjure with.

The first musical that I ever attended
Filled my rib cage with such a feeling
I had never experienced before
That was Paradise

The first time my man took me in his arms
For our very first kiss
And I realised that he was the one for me
That was Paradise

Our Wedding day, the sun pouring
Through the Altar window,
Shining on all our friends
That's Paradise

Holding newborn children of our own
Day dreaming about their lives,
Who they looked like and who they would be
One day when they were grown
That was Paradise too

Paradise is not just a place in heaven
It can be wherever we want it to be
It is heaven in a place on earth
Not just a figment of our imagination

First Kiss

It was a lovely summers day
We lay there rolling on the grass
It is such a long, long time ago
I don't recall how it came to pass

I can only just remember
what it was that Mummy said
Some time later on that day
when she tucked me up in bed

She said we've had a lovely day
And taken lots of pictures
Daddy was being mischievous
And spoke to Mummy in whispers.

It seemed that little Tommy
had lost his heart you see
And that first kiss was meant to show
That he'd given it to me.

It was many years afterwards
When my fiancé came to tea
That daddy brought those pictures out
For the entire world to see.

'So that was how it came to pass'
My Boyfriend said to me
'Kissing lads in Armley Park
When you were only three!'

First Love

Last night I held a young man in my arms.
He held my hand, we danced, we kissed
And I succumbed to his charms.
It was only then that Rachel appeared,
her baby boy to seek.
This young man that I was dancing with
was none other than her son Alfie,
His age? Just seven weeks!

The Little One

Little One, you're all alone
Sitting on Mummy's bed.
She's fast asleep, no one to call
You're too young to know she is dead

You run your hands through her silver hair,
Please Mummy, will you wake up.
You don't have a Daddy that you can call
You never had a daddy at all

Little one what will happen to you?
When people find you there
Will you find yourself in an orphanage?
With all your emotions lay bare?

There's no one left to hug you,
And tuck you in each night
To put their arms around you
And say I love you darling,
Goodnight

No one to see you growing up
As the child becomes a girl
The first time you go on a date
And your heart is in a whirl

Nobody there to see you
When you walk down the aisle
No Mum or Dad to share your life
Not even the day you became a wife

You never had a Grandma
She died before you were born
What kind of Mum could bear a child?
Then leave her all alone.

When you conceive your first born
That feeling is just great
But to become a mother at
Seventy-two
Isn't that just a little too late?

Further thoughts on
'The Little One'

I'm not sure how to feel about
Having the oldest Mummy!!
Both of us incontinent
And both of us are gummy

Contributed by
Ashley Crompton

Valentine

It's many years since first we met
And you've always been my girl
Through the years it's grown better yet,
and my heart is still in a whirl
Together we watched our love unfurl
into such a wonderful thing

How could we know what a precious pearl
The passing years would bring
Being with you gas given me
a lifetime full of pleasure
Since the day you said that you'd be mine
my dearest sweetest. Valentine

My Gift for You

Accept this little gift of mine
A souvenir of my love for you
A precious gift to help you through
As you walk the paths of life

Whether you are here at home
Or very far away
Remember that my love for you
Is with you all the way

Please accept these simple things
They hold my heart and all my love
And know that every time you touch them
They came to you with all my love

The Christening Gown

It was just an ordinary christening gown
White satin, and trimmed with lace
Handed down through generations
The kind you cannot replace

It was passed down through generations
Handled with love and care
The kind of thing one cherished
In memory of those who are no longer here

The last baby who wore it was Daddy,
He was killed in Afghanistan
His son would have wanted to know him
And now he never can

The one before him was Grandpa,
Who died in the second world war.
The very first baby to wear it was
Great grandpa, who fell in the one before

It is a wonderful thing tradition
Remembering those who lived here before
But sad, so very sad to lose them
Because of a bloody war

Is this all our loved ones are here for
All that our children are worth
Destined to die fighting
To give others Peace on Earth?

The Red Balloon

The little girl held on tightly
To her beautiful red balloon.
She was on her way back
From a birthday party,
And would be home quite soon.

She skipped along the pathway
The balloon high above her head.
She never saw the car
As it mounted the pavement,
And the next minute she was dead.

Everyone said that Angela
Was much too young to die.
The big balloon carefully picked her up
And they floated off into the sky.

They all knew that Angela
Had been carried off to heaven,
High up over the moon.
Evermore to play with the Angels
And her beautiful red balloon

Forever Young

(In memory of Marylin)

My friend I beg you not to fear
The ending of your life.
The time when you must leave
Your husband or your wife.

Just be aware that when
You reach the heavens above
You will be reunited with everyone
That you have ever loved.

And when your soul mate
comes to you at last.
Then will be the time for you
To forget the sadness of the past.

On that wonderful day
Those glorious bells will be rung
And from that time on
You will remain **Forever Young.**

Health and Well Being

So you have a medical condition
that plays havoc with your health.
you were never fortunate enough
To have been crowned by wealth.

In spite of this you have been blessed
with the unique gift of choice.
'There isn't anything I cannot do'
Says that inwardly small voice.

There is nothing that you cannot do
To live your life of bliss
Who knows what dizzy heights
You can attain if you remember this.

The phrase 'Life is for living'
Is very, very true so why not
don your thinking cap and
Make it work for you?

You can do any thing you want to
within your disability, as long
as you remember to work,
within the realms of your capabilities

Phoebe

Darling girl, I am so sorry
That I can't be with you on this
your naming day
But in my heart I shall be with you
Even though I'm faraway

As you journey through your life
There will be such wonderful things
Like the glorious sunshine that a new day brings
And the cooing of doves as they flap their wings.

The heavenly look on a little ones face
or the rush of a waterfall in some quiet place
The sound of the rain on your window pane
Or the sight of the rainbow when it appears again

All these things are a part of your life
On your journey each day as a child, teenager, wife.
We learn to appreciate the things that we love
These heaven sent gifts that come down from above

My First Rose

Tenderly I caress the petals
of my very first rose
A gift for me by the man
who chose me for his wife

The bud is darkly red and deep
Like velvet to the touch
It's stem is tall and strong
Just as the man to whom
one day I shall belong

The dearest man with whom
I wish to share my life
Who means so much that
One day soon I shall be his wife

Two years have come gone
and I am in a daze
Today will be the happiest of days
Because it is our wedding day

I look at those roses in my bouquet
I have no wish to throw them away
Even if they be caught by a future Bride
So happy with her young man by her side

Yet if my flowers can bring such bliss
within another love so true
Perhaps she will remember this
As she lifts her face, for her lovers next kiss

My Memory

The most important thing to me
Is of course my memory
It helps me know just who I am,
What I do, where I am.

Everything that I do and say
Those memories of yesterday
And all those dear ones
Now passed away

It helps me to forget those times.
Too painful to remember
And all those happier things
Like Christmas in December

Of all the things there are in life
That means the world to me
The last thing I would want to lose
Is my memory

Yet most of all it means to me
Whatever else I do
My memories are always there,
Whenever I think of you

Me, Myself and I

I used to be so lonely
When my husband went away
I used to sit and wonder how,
I would survive each day.

Then one day I looked into a mirror
And stopped to wonder why
I'd ever felt alone at all,
When there is Me, Myself and I

Now whenever I go anywhere
I never go alone,
Me and myself are with me
The loneliness has gone

When we go out shopping
There's always someone new to see
they could be our latest friends
Him, himself and he

Our lives have been linked
for many a year
There's been love and laughter
And sometimes a tear

There's often been squabbles;
Though I don't know why
In the in the lives of
Me myself and I

I don't know how long
We can go on, along this road
we've stepped upon
It could be that we shall be
Together 'til we die
The intrepid me myself, and I

On Blackpool Beach

At this place where the sky meets the sea
It is as calm as calm can be
The tide creeps over the silver sand
This is our home, our England

Now the tide has turned, covering the shore
The waters are not serene any more
Pushed forward by the prevailing wind
The passion of the seas unwind

The sky grows dark and stormy
The angry waves lash the shore
The weather is cold, the wind blows strong
This phase can't last for long

The weather has been so adverse
Whilst we've been holidaying here
What if there's flooding on the promenade?
This is our greatest fear

Those grey and vicious waters
Have such a hefty crashing sound
It makes the visitors quite cautious
Of the flooding all around

Now look once more, the tide has turned
The waves retreating out to sea
Now as we stroll along the beach
All is peace and harmony

Soon the tide will turn once more
And the cycle begins again
The sea will battle with the shore
Until peace reigns once again

Snapshots

Snapshots unlike memories
Never ever fade
Wedding pictures still as fresh
as the day our vows were made.

Days will grow shorter as the years pass by
Yet your image remains the same
Unlike me you will never grow old
Grey haired and wrinkled as the days unfold

We that are left might mellow with age
Just as the ink on these pages will fade
But I shall never forget
those vows that we made

Life from now on could become
Quite insane
Yet the face in the picture
will remain the same

My Silent World

I live within a silent world
A place that's mine alone
It can be a cold and lonely place
That few have ever known

It has been with me all my life
Since I was but a child
When I grew up and fell in love
My crazy world went wild

With such love and tenderness
That he has always shown to me
I realised how wonderful
My silent world could be

Whenever I look into his eyes
Or at the expression on his face
My lonely world just comes to life
And my understanding finds it's place

The years have passed and now at last
We have children of our own
I can never hear their laughter
But I can see when the tears fall down

I lock them away in my special world
And find solutions for their fears
Until the laughter I have shared with them
Soothes away their tears

We are a happy family as everyone can see
But no matter what the future brings
Some things can never be and no one
Can ever take my silent world from me

Transport

Like everyone in the world today
I use transport every day
It may not be the traditional kind
I can travel the world within my mind

I sit down after a hard days work
My imagination does not shirk
I am transported far and wide
To every corner of the countryside

Sometimes it's an island in the sun
Visited and loved by everyone
Some days I travel to the Heavens above
To be reunited with those that I love

Taken to the days that used to be
When you shared this earth with me
I am content, not often sad
And so thankful for all that I've had

I have my imagination to transport me
Any place in the universe I choose to be
This type of travel is for everyone,
Traffic jam free, and lots of fun

Holidays

There are many, many special days
Like Christmas day and Easter day
Just think of all the Birthdays,
And none of these are holidays.

Mums are just too happy
To leave the kitchen sink
The washing and the ironing
So much harder than you think

The cooking and the cleaning
. Make their lives a bore
They really need a holiday
Upon some distant shore

The Guys who do the plumbing,
Roofing, and such like,
Can't wait for clocking off time
To climb upon their bikes.

Our girls work in the office
Their job is such a pain
They can't wait to grab the chance
To get upon a plane

At last the holidays are here,
We are so eager to get away
Can't wait to get our bags packed
At last we're on our way

Some of us are flying off,
To explore those distant lands,
While others are just as happy
Lazing on the sands

For two short weeks you are free
There is so much to do and see
Whatever it is you choose to do
Your holiday is down to you.

Go out fishing, take a swim
Or spend a couple of days at the gym.
Forget the boss, your time is yours
Someone else can do his chores.

All too soon the time has gone
And once again we're back at home
Time to forget the holiday scene
Now we are back in the work routine.

Now it's time to take a coffee break,
To show off the pictures you like to take,
Memories that you hold dear,
Until you go back again next year

The Money Box

There is a little money box
That I've had all my life
From Infancy and Adolescence
To Teenager and Wife

Now I am a Widow
I still have that little box
Built just like a little house
It has a door that locks

There is a little person
Who sits outside the house
Holding a plate between his hands
His name is Mickey Mouse

If you would like to
Put a smile upon his face
You only have to place a coin
On that little plate

If you push him forward
From his elbow
until his figure locks
Then he will tip your money
Through the letter box

I still have this little box
I use it to this day
And when I get a two pound coin
He still comes out to play

The Public House

I know a little Public House
Next door to the Railway Station
It's just the place to stop a while
Once you've reached your destination

It's built from railway carriages
Which add up to three
The bar is smart and up to date
And the lounge has it's own T.V.

It is always very busy with people
who are waiting for their trains
Not to mention those who call in
On their way back home again

With it's hanging baskets, and seats outside
Local folks like it a lot
Over the years it has become known
As the "Coronation Scot"

The Carrier Bag

It was just a plain old carrier bag
filled with her worldly goods.
Two dresses and a pinny,
and an old-fashioned pixie hood.

She set it down upon the floor,
after the men were gone.
It was Christmas Eve at last,
and she was left on her own.

She thought back to the morning
when the bailiffs came along'
Knowing that when they did come
she would have neither house nor home

She walked through the hall to let the men in,
But just to be sure they hammered again
"I'll be there in a minute" she began to call out,
Bailiffs know what's to do and they don't hang about.

They took her possessions and put them out in the yard.
Her life this past year had been very hard.
Her husband was dead and her children all gone
And she never got used to living alone.

That very same day came the final blow,
A letter arrived from her boss to say;
We have to tell you your job has to go
There is no option the firm closes today.

As she locked the door and posted the key
She was well aware that there was little to see
Of the life she had lived with the man she had wed
This is how it must be, there's no more to be said.

She picked up the carrier bag without making a sound
As she looked down on the path she saw a pound
She hadn't any money so this was real treasure
On what to spend it she would decide at her leisure

She walked down the road not knowing where to turn
The coin in her pocket was beginning to burn
I know, what I'm going to do with it
I am going to buy a lottery ticket

Needless to say she had bought a winner
Now she was sure she could afford to by dinner
She went back to the shop to collect her lot
It was there that she learned she had won the jackpot

So now our friend is a millionaire
Who can face every day without worry or care
But one thing that she will never regret
Is that pound on the floor which paid for her bet

The Iceberg

She stands there cool, in white.
She's always the same be it day or night
Her image is cool and serene as the sea
Too cold for comfort she appears to be

Her face is white as she faces the sun
I have never seen her, this beautiful one
There have been lots of pictures of her 'tis true
I'd like to see her when she comes into view

She lives far away in a remote place you see
And it isn't somewhere that I'd like to be
Such a long way to go, or so I've been told
It's no easy journey when you're growing old

She stands there in her glory, for all to see
Quite a legend she has turned out to be
So many men have succumbed to her charms
She welcomes them all with open arms

Standing there before them a vision in ice
The men in her life don't often think twice
Enticed to a rock by a sudden upsurge
She's beat them again this icy iceberg

Trees

Tall, majestic, strong and free
Is the magic of a tree
In springtime filled with blossoms
That are beyond belief
Full of glorious splendour
As they lay beside the leaf

Trees give us the summer shade
In some quiet leafy glade
Where we sit and take the time
To see and hear the magic rhyme
That is the tree

The birds that fill the tree with song
Make us want to sing along
Fluttering through majestic boughs
While the daylight hour allows

All too soon the winter comes
And all the leaves are shed
All the summer flowers
Are now in their wintry beds

The tree still holds it's head up high
Against the grey and wintry sky
When springtime comes around again
And the buds are bursting green
In perfect majesty

We look forward to those sunny days
When we will sit with ease
And bask within the glory
Of our beautiful trees.

Rainbows

Rain filled skies, dark and grey,
Another wet and miserable day.
In no time at all the sun breaks through,
No more rain for an hour or two.
Beautiful skies and a rainbow for you
Over the hills we see those glorious colours
Warming the skies and waking the flowers
Sunshine and raindrops, and the rainbow is ours.
Red is the colour that forms the very first arch
Orange follows on swift and smart.
Yellow comes next to complete the view
Followed by beautiful green and blue
Indigo and violet complete the set
A more beautiful rainbow I have never
Seen yet

Christine & Janet

To replace the tomato
That you never took,
I'm giving you this little book.
If you should read
Each day around three
Maybe sometimes
you will think of me
There's just one thing before I go
This comes with love
From Auntie Mo.

Sometimes At Dawn

Sometimes at dawn
I awaken to your voice.
In the stillness of the morn
you call out to me,

As though I have a
chance to speak with you.
On this brand new day
I can't believe that so much time
has slipped away.

In all the years that you were here,
You lived so far away,
I never saw your face or heard you speak.
We always had so much to say.

And now my unseen friend;
You are but a memory.
Just now, for us there is no choice
And I must wait to hear your voice,
If Heaven can wait awhile

The Home of Inspiration

Biscuits are sweet things, very nice to eat
Sitting at this table where we all meet
As we sit and write we enjoy our cup of tea
Along with a biscuit or two, sometimes it's three

Our brains may become rusted as time moves along
Yet we all can remember the lines of any old song
"It is no secret" we have all heard of this
And what of the other one "Memories are made of this"

We can all raise our glasses to the years we have shared
Writing and chatting, no subject being spared
If we have a windfall perhaps that day will be
The time to publish our work, just you wait and see

It could be tomorrow or in years yet to come
But until that day happens we'll have lots of fun
We're all collectors of dreams don't you know
And when we write, the words we've collected will show

If you want to make a name for yourself
Don't put your talent away on the shelf
Go to your brain factory and start right away
We know there's no tomorrow, so let's live for today

The Language of the Rings

When I was young he gave me a ring
With just a single diamond in
I hope one day you will be "Mine"
You'll always be my valentine

A few years later the ring had two
"Be mine" is still my wish for you
Three diamonds this time just for
You, simply to say that "I love You"

Decision time now, this was a sign
Four diamonds say "Will you be mine?"
Then came the best day of my life, darling
Girl "Will you be my wife?"

Fifty years have come and gone sadly now
I live alone and many's the time I wonder how
Such love could last a lifetime through and
Remembered he always said to me

You are the "Dearest" thing in the world you see
This was the last ring that he gave to me
Diamond Emerald Amethyst Ruby Emerald Sapphire Turquoise

A Birth, Marriage And Death in a Day

A birth, marriage and death in a day,
It's amazing how quickly time slips away.
What will become of the child that is born
At the first sign of light in the early morn?

What of the lovers so keen to be wed
Who married at noon it has to be said
They planned to fly out to their honeymoon isle
The perfect start to a marriage with style

Later that evening, cold and alone
an old man lay dying in his lonely old home.
There are no loving arms to hold him
as his journey begins, only a priest who listens
while he repents for his sins.

He lay there peacefully, reflecting his life,
He had no brothers or sisters, not even a wife
A church bell tolled the midnight hour
As the old man died just seconds before

The Ancient Toad

The ancient toad had a big long nose
that he poked into everything.
Not only that, this big fat lad
didn't just croak he could sing.

Every day he would go out to play
and croak away until nightfall,
but as soon as the moon
Rose high in the sky, he would
sing out an Indian love call.

He consoled himself by the
light of the moon,
singing out songs to the skies.
When suddenly he was being raised up,
'til his gaze met those beautiful eyes.

A pair of red lips then rested on his
In a kiss just fit for a prince
He had waited so long for
some wonderful miss
to bring him alive just like this.

Now at last it had happened
having waited so long,
It felt like since time had begun.
He took the girl in his arms
using all of his charms
For he was no longer a Toad
but a Man

Betrayal

I am devastated. How does anyone
Carry on alone? I peel and portion
A tangerine, thinking all the while
About the love that I lost.

He was my life. I spit the first of the
Pips toward the bin, it misses.
He betrayed me; there goes another pip
The juice is alien to my tongue.

Why did he have to take her in our bed?
I spit another pip viciously this time.
The juice from the tangerine
Is acid as the pain that I feel.

What to do now; pick myself up,
Get my hair done; buy a new dress.
The world is not spacious enough
For my grief. Smile begin again
I'm going out now

Bath Night

There once was a little girl
Who hated having a bath.
Everyone guessed what was going on
If they happened walked up the path.

Mother worried about her daughter
Who was growing up with this fear of water
Until one night or so it seemed
A still small voice broke into her dreams.

"Now then Mother, listen hear
From now on you have nothing to fear
I have found the answer to all your troubles
Just fill your daughters bath with bubbles."

The next day when it was time for the bath
Mummy smiled when her girl began to laugh
"Just look at all the bubbles in here
There's enough to hide in until next year."

"I don't think you'll need to do that" Mummy said
"In another ten minutes it will be time for bed"
When she climbed into the bath she heard
a voice say "At least you came to see me today."

There at the other end of the bath
a boy made of bubbles was making her laugh
He had great big blue eyes and white frothy hair
All that the poor girl could do was stare

"If Mum finds you in here you'll be in trouble."
"Don't be so daft I'm only a bubble
I'll hide under the water you wait and see
If she comes in later she'll not see me"

Later that night as she climbed into bed
"Oh Mum I've had such fun" she said
"we have been playing at doubles.
Me and my new pal Michael Bubbles"

Birthdays

What is it that everyone has
That cannot be given away?
Something that will stay with us
Until our dying day.

No one can take it from us
Of that there is no doubt
It was bestowed on us when we
were born and will remain till we go out

There are those who are underprivileged
And those who are well to do
And yet everyone has got one
Folks like me and you

None of us have more of than one
But this day still comes to you
Unless of course you are the Queen
Who just happens to have two

We never forget those special days
Of the ones that we hold dear
And remember their anniversaries
Every single year

Darkness

Through the darkness
Your voice is reaching out to me
The darkness envelops the sound
Into a low husky tone.

I call out you name
But still I cannot see you
I long to touch your face
And hold your hand

But wait! Here a light
Penetrates the darkness
I can see the shape of you
Against the night sky

Now it is gone!
As swiftly as it came
I call your name once more
And still there is no reply
I am alone again

Elusive Information

Barbara's searching frantically
For a truly British ditty,
It may be that it's quite serious,
Or possibly quite witty.

Written to help remember
Our royal Kings and Queens,
The dates of their accession,
And demise so it would seem.

She has written to some magazines
To enlist the public's help,
As far as a reply's concerned—
There's not a single yelp.

Surely there is someone,
Who knows the poem she seeks
She's beginning to despair
As the days turn into weeks.

Because out there in Australia
The information's not to hand
She hoped to find an answer
Over here in England.

So come on you British poets
And citizens alike,
Do as the politician says
And get up on your bike.

Let us try and help our Barbara
find the elusive ode,
Brush up on all our memory banks,
and get into history mode!

Evening Dress

He wore a dashing white tuxedo,
With trousers that were black as the night.
Just like the bow tie, he wore next to his shirt
that was crisply starched and white.

He appeared the door with a red
rose in his hand,
At the home of his lady love.
as he stood there waiting for a response,
He thanked the good Lord above.

The door opened wide, he was ushered
inside, And shown to a seat in the hall.
Before very long she appeared by his side,
Wearing a smile that was envied by all

So glad was he to be given this chance,
He had loved her so long from afar.
After all this long wait, today was the date
He would take her along to the dance.

She should have known there was no cause to fret,
For they'd both had the time of their life.
The night was all set to become better yet,
when he proposed to make her his wife.

The Long Light Shines

It was early in the year
At a place I had never been before
A village warm and welcoming
Like the ever open door

At first glance I fell in love
With this pretty little place
On an evening like this I did not
have far to look for a friendly face

I did not have to seek
the way I did before,
surrounded by these folks,
with arms held out in welcome,
like an ever open door

Cars are stopping in the lane
And still the rain comes down
Those country lanes are waterlogged
And I am Frightened

Children and adults alike
Are screaming as they become trapped
The water tumbles over their vehicles
Swallowing them in their wake
And I am frightened

Now the torrent is out of control
Invading the homes of people
There is panic, screaming, shouting
And I am frightened

Suddenly everything has changed
The long light shines across the lake
And still the rain pours down
And I am frightened

The storm has passed and life
Goes on the way it was before
And once again the village
offers an ever open door,
And I am no longer frightened

Easter Time

At last the spring is here once more,
and Easter is upon us.
The daffodils are coming out
and rabbits start a playing

Trees and flowers begin to grow,
and before too long
The world will know
it's Eastertide once more

The clocks have changed and days grow long
And the birds are bursting into song
The children play and dance with glee
Around the Maypole for all to see

With winter far behind us
And good weather still to come
There will be lots of gardening
And picnics going on

Then all too soon school holidays are here
The children are so delighted
No more school for six whole weeks
But Mums aren't too excited

Before too long the summers gone
The nights are getting longer
There's bonfire chumping to be done
And fireworks to buy

Now Christmas is upon us
and it's wintertime once more
with snowmen and roasted chestnuts
And presents by the score

And then before we know it
Before we know quite where we are
The trees and flowers show us
That it's Easter time once more

Fifteen Sunflowers

Vincent was a clever man
His gifts were manifold
And the talent that was his
Was a great joy to behold.

In a field outside his home
Of sunflowers it was full.
With long green stems,
Dark brown hearts
And petals gold as the sun.

Vincent had a heart so good
Their beauty could not be denied
He could not ignore these flowers
Even if he tried.

Then came the day he went outside
and chose fifteen of the best
He put them in an earthenware vase
Their beauty did the rest

He took some paint and an easel
And set to work for hours and hours
Until at last it was finished
The painting we all know as
SUNFLOWERS

My English Teacher

I had an English Teacher
Who I liked very much.
She was very, very special
And we always kept in touch.

The best thing that she gave to me
Was a lasting love of poetry
She taught me how to write in rhyme
And always seemed to have the time

Some of the poems that she taught me
I can remember them by heart
And even when I write today
She always plays a part.

And when the children misbehaved
She knew just how to stop them
A very strict no nonsense type
Our very dear Miss Topham

Graffiti

How much do we really know
About this passion that folks hate so much?
It seems to be something that Teenagers do
And helps them keep in touch

They seem to get busy with several spray cans
and any brick wall that is bare
Whilst the old folk class them as vandals
Complaining that it just isn't fair.

Then all at once we have a cleanup campaign
Just to keep them out of their hair
But if we step back and look for a moment
A lot of their work is quite good

Don't be too quick to condemn them
Let us give them a wall of their own
Then maybe, just maybe one day
We'll have a genius all our own

Grandparents

Quite often these days I seem to be
Locked within my memory.
Remembering Sunday visits as a child,
Expected to behave so meek and mild.

We never left our Heavenly Father in the lurch,
So every Sunday we went to church.
From there, straight on to Grandma's house
As quietly as a real church mouse

We always looked forward to grandma's lunch,
A full roast dinner for us to munch.
Aunties Uncles and Cousins too,
All waiting to meet around half past two.

Even though times were hard, Grandpa
still had his job in the old mill yard.
And even though he was always willing,
He worked jolly hard to earn his shilling.

Then at last when everyone had gone
Gran and I sat on our own,
With the very best pastime that you ever saw
Grandmas very own magic jig-saw.

Grandma's Kitchen

My Grandmas kitchen was old and worn
Just like the wainscot that hugged the wall
It was always warm and welcoming to me
As comforting as a hot cup of tea.

I remember the home made bread
that Gran used to bake, not to mention
her mouth watering chocolate cake
That she baked for tea in the afternoon

We used to visit each day around noon
Our Gran never seemed to tire
We used to play on the old clipped rugs
While the kettle purred on the fire

Gran was always so busy on baking day
she never had much time for games
But later on when her work was done
She always made sure we had lots of fun

Hogmanay

Now it is time to celebrate
the last day of the year
If you happen to be in Scotland
Then you are sure to hear
The bells that ring when the Scotsmen sing
And the bagpipes play along

When it comes to midnight
and the bells begin to chime
A dark handsome man is first in line
When the folks all go first footing
They all have a jolly good time
And there's never any looting

Everyone's out bearing their gifts
There's a slice of black bun, just for fun
And a lump of coal, with salt
And if that's not followed by shortbread
and whisky, then someone is at fault

And when the celebrations are over
Comes the greeting between you and me
"A guid New Year to one and A'
And many may ye see"

Halloween

The first day of November
we all know as All Saints Day.
A time to celebrate the lives
Of those Saints who came our way.

But first we remember the witches
who fly beyond the moon
and the ghouls and ghosts, and beasties,
Who all come out too soon.

This horrid combination
emerge at Halloween
With their magic spells and witchcraft
The like you've never seen

Just before midnight when their job is done
The magic all gone too soon
If you look at the sky very closely
You can see witches flying over the moon

They fill the sky when All Saints Day is nigh
All quick to make their escape
I don't understand why they are so underhand
Maybe some one can tell me why

Holidays

There are many, many special days
Like Christmas day and Easter day
Just think of all the Birthdays,
And none of these are holidays.

Mums are just too happy
To leave the kitchen sink
The washing and the ironing
So much harder than you think

The cooking and the cleaning
. Make their lives a bore
They really need a holiday
Upon some distant shore

The Guys who do the plumbing,
Roofing, and such like,
Can't wait for clocking off time
To climb upon their bikes.

Our girls work in the office
Their job is such a pain
They can't wait to grab the chance
To get upon a plane

At last the holidays are here,
We are so eager to get away
Can't wait to get our bags packed
At last we're on our way

Some of us are flying off,
To explore those distant lands,
While others are just as happy
Lazing on the sands

For two short weeks you are free
There is so much to do and see
Whatever it is you choose to do
Your holiday is down to you.

Go out fishing, take a swim
Or spend a couple of days at the gym.
Forget the boss, your time is yours
Someone else can do his chores.

All too soon the time has gone
And once again we're back at home
Time to forget the holiday scene
Now we are back in the work routine.

Now it's time to take a coffee break,
To show off the pictures you like to take,
Memories that you hold dear,
Until you go back again next year

Just An Old Thing

It's only just an old thing
I heard someone say
A simple little memory
Saved from yesterday

It was just a little something
that I couldn't throw away
Because every time I tried to
I always heard you say
that one day soon, we would have
another special day

A piece of lacy nonsense
A saucy bit of stuff
Cheeky sparkly underwear
Never quite enough

White bows held it together
This cheeky bit of lace
But it didn't quite hide enough
To stop the smile that crossed your face

When it came to foreplay
I was really quite a dunce
But knew enough to realise
That all your birthday's
had come at once

Light of my Life

When you said to me 'You are the light of my life'
I immediately asked you to become my wife
The happiness that I began to feel suddenly
Became so unreal it was just as though
Life had lifted a veil

But once again I am living in the past
The way that you felt just didn't last
For more than just a month or two
And then you said 'I can no longer live with you

So here I am living in a cavity so vast
Grieving for a love that just couldn't last
Now all I am left with is to say
Where is my love from yesterday?

Laura

Little one, with eyes of blue
Angelic child that has come t o you
Ultimate joy to you she will bring,
Reality is, she will make your heart sing

A tiny child born out of love
Sent to you from heaven above
Teach her all the little things
you learned at mothers knee

Enjoy lots of hugs and kisses,
and happy she will be
Make sure that she has lots of space
when it's time to play

Pretend games will be different
every time she comes to stay
Expect the unexpected,
it's the only thing to do,

She will be sure to let you know
she thinks the world of you
That will also be the time
she knows you love her too!

Emotions

Happiness is loving
And being loved in return
Sorrow is something
that we all have to learn
There is no way of knowing
when love will depart
Or the sorrow that comes
with a broken heart
Bitterness will only
add to the pain
Bringing back sorrow
again and again
Life is too short
to live with regret
We have to move on
There's a happier life yet

The Shout

Sitting there at the big brown desk
Her ideas like rapid fire
The words kept coming thick and fast
'Til she began to tire

She put the pen down on the table
There was nothing left to say.
She had been writing since early morning
Such a long, long day.

Next she donned her hat and coat
Placed a flower at her throat.
Whatever happened she must not be late
And set out to meet her date.

Stepping out on to the street
She spied the guy she was to meet.
She only meant to call his name
And raised her voice to call out
When all at once the call became
A lusty full blown shout

Queen of the Night

Sleek and slender, hair black and shiny;
Eyes the greenest you have ever seen.
If her gaze should happen to fall on you,
Their scrutiny becomes so keen

Her beautiful eyes take on the
Appearance of slits, in her small pointed face.
Her appearance often meant to deceive.
This feisty individual has style and grace
When she finally makes her choice

Oh Boy! That is something else.
Their lovemaking is as noisy as it is passionate,
Often deep guttural sounds will escape
From their throats as the passion grows.

Once a Mother she lost a great deal
Of the wild child image
And was much more subdued,
Choosing to spend most of her time
Hunting and foraging for food,

Always fiercely protective of her young,
It is woe betide anyone or anything
That tries to come between them.
One false move and she will scratch
The eyes out of any one of her enemies.

As soon as her offspring were
Old enough to fend for themselves
She had no qualms about leaving
Them to take up her old life again

"La Gioconda"

Everyone has heard of "Mona Lisa"
The girl with the enigmatic smile
Being painted by "Da Vinci"
Had made her life worthwhile.

To be portrayed all those years ago
In fifteen hundred and four
Has meant she has been remembered
So often, and so much more

Where she lived at home on Italy
She was known as "La Gioconda"
Why her smile was so enigmatic
Has made many people wonder.

Anyone who has ever seen her smile
Will never forget the "Mona Lisa"
Even though this special picture of her
Has been around for such a long, long while

The Letter

The envelope dropped to the floor
New Zealand calling out once more
My friend has been there for many years
we've shared our tears and our laughter
And sometimes our fears

We first met at primary school
When we were only four
And always been the best of friends
Now who could ask for more

When we grew up and married
That was the time she went away
More years than I can remember
have passed since that sad day

I don't often get a letter
When she wants to tell the tale
It's more likely to arrive on the air waves
I think it's called email

I wonder why she felt the need
To write to me this time?
I know that it's so unusual
I shall have to reply in rhyme

Surprise, surprise, this letter
Is such a special Tome
Daphne is writing to tell me
That at last she is coming home

The Yellow Automobile

We loved our smart new automobile
From the day we brought it home
A beautiful yellow convertible
The best car we ever owned

With a canvas top that rolled right back
And seats of the finest green
It truly was the greatest car
that we had ever seen

It carried us to work each day
And brought us back each night
With it's hood rolled down
and the wind in our hair
We must have looked a sight

When the weekends came around again
We 'd found a good way to lighten our load
We had such fun in those far off days
As once again we took to the road

Once in our lives it was here to stay
The love had set the seal
From hereon in life would always be good
In our beautiful automobile

The Great Yorkshire Show

I've never been to the Yorkshire Show
It's not a place I ever wanted to go
But when we were asked to write about it today
I hadn't a clue what I was going to say

I went home and did some research that night
To see what went on and find out if I might
Be interested in going along to see
All the exciting things there are going to be.

Apart from the agricultural shows
The cattle the pigs and the sheep
You can spend all day, stroll round with ease.
You can surely find something there
that will please

There's motor cross and falconry
A cheese and dairy show
There are even show jumpers
Who are prepared to take a bow

So tonight I'm going on the net
To view, and book my ticket
With all the things that are going on
There might even be game of cricket

The Stripper

She donned her bra and nylons,
Suspenders in disarray
She was so impatient
Must not be late today

She sat before the mirror,
Her cosmetics to apply.
There really wasn't time to wait
for her eyelashes to dry

She dabbed her perfume here and there
And at last behind her ears
Then one last glance toward the clock
Confirmed her greatest fear

If she did not hurry,
And get into her dress
The interviews would be over
Then she'd be in a mess

She walked into the office
Still struggling with her zipper
The man just looked and said
It was last week we interviewed
For Strippers

The Waterfall

I stood close to the rocks
behind the waterfall,
All was quiet and still.
The water like a sheet of ice
And the world was cold and chill

The waterfall is hanging
shining in the winter sun.
crystal clear and sparkling,
On earth since time begun

A frosty window on the world.
Waiting for spring to arrive
like a Saviour long expected
To bring the whole world alive

And now at last the spring has come
The earth reborn once more
the water freed and rushing down
The way it did before

Dragon flies and fishes are
leaping to greet the spring
Once again she works her magic
And makes the whole world sing

Chairman of the Board

A Memo to all the members regarding the AGM

The Chairman of the Board
Has given his word
That as the company
Is doing so well at present,
Employees who are present
At the meeting will all
Receive a present.

It is hoped that the Lord Mayor
Will also be present at the meeting.
At present we are awaiting
Confirmation that his Lordship will
Indeed be present for the presentation.
If the Mayor agrees to be present
He will be the one to present
The presents to all those
Who are present at that time.

When the presentations
Have been completed,
The Chairman will present
The Lord Mayor with one of our
Vehicles as a thank you present
For being present at our meeting.
In view of the fact that
He is so busy himself at present
We are sure that his present
Will be much appreciated.

(Footnote) Fourteen Members were present

The other side of the Story

Mary, Mary was always contrary,
She met her Fella each day in the dairy.
Until she chucked her amorous lover,
When they were caught by her angry Mother.

Jack and Jill went up the hill
Though it was not to get the water.
All was fine until Jack met Jill,
Who was the Vicars daughter!

Humpty Dumpty fell of the wall
For one of the Kings own men.
He did not fancy the others at all,
But he still kept an eye on them.

It was Jack Spratt who ate all the fat
Yet his wife was always so mean
But silly old Jack in spite of all that
Always treated her like a Queen

Red Riding Hood was not very good,
And neither was Cinderella.
If ever you saw them out in the wood
To be sure they'd be meeting a Fella.

Fairy tales are all very well
For folks like me and you.
To keep us happy truth to tell,
Even though they're not always true.

A Trip Into The Country

Tomorrow is a very special day
Already I have packed my bags
And put the printer and my laptop away
And just in case you haven't guessed
Tomorrow begins my holiday

I have travelled to places far and wide
But this time I shall explore the countryside
Where mountains high and rivers deep
Provide a haven to wild life, fast asleep

Along the moors the heathers grow
In bright array their colours show
While up in the skies the starling flies
Soaring above the trees so green
A more beautiful sight I have never seen.

High in the mountains and the hills
These glorious places I love to roam
And even though I travel alone
Perhaps there are others just like me
Who love the chance to be wild and free

Now is the time to travel once more
Beside the sea, the sand and shore
And for now I no longer wish to roam
For me there is no place like home

Now I am back in my own space
No one knows how much I love this place
This comfy haven when my travels are done
A lovely home built just for one

Tomorrow I shall write another rhyme
Telling about the next time
That I shall pack and go away
On another country holiday

High Heels

I love my pair of high-heeled shoes
Specially made to get rid of the blues.
Every time I get the chance
I don my shoes then go out to a dance.
It's guaranteed I shall have a good time
I'm not the kind to sit at home and pine.
And when the weekend comes along
I shall be back where I belong
Out on the dance floor singing the blues,
In those black and shiny high heeled shoes

In My Magic Box

I will put in the box
Blue moods and sadness
mixed with joy and laughter,
and the smile of the Madonna.

I will put in the box
A memory of my first day at school
a slate to write upon,
and sleeps in the afternoons.

I will put in the box
The rattle of looms in the mill
girls in their black pinnies,
and barges chugging up the canal.

I will put in the box
All my hopes, dreams and wishes
the ones that came true.
The ones that gave me you,
and all the thrills that came after.

My box will be made from
all my treasured memories.
Woven with moonbeams
and stars to light my way
through the darkness.

There will be faces and places
that I have never seen
waiting for me in every corner,
so then I can play catch up
with the dream.
Written in the style of Kit Wright

Leisure

What is leisure?
It is my life and my pleasure
Each day is a treasure for me.

I can live for each day
Always make time to play
For life is so precious you see.

Whether it is to work or to play
Just being here every day
Means everything to me

There are things in my past
That were not meant to last
And death came too close for me

But since my time is not now
I can try to show how
I can live each day as my last

My Ukulele

I have always loved my ukulele
I've had it quite a while
Bought for me by my Mother
When I was but a child.

I learned to play my ukulele
When I was only three
And entertained our relatives
When they came round to tea

It has the name George Formby
written on the case
I have not heard his name before
or even seen his face

If he enjoyed the playing
With only half the fun
Maybe he wowed his audiences
As much as I have done

It is my life's ambition
To play before the Queen
At the most successful concert
The world has ever seen

Maybe one day I'll get the chance
To play Wembley arena
And when that happy day arrives
I shall become the greatest Diva

Fame is not the most important thing
As I'm sure you all will know
To play gives me such pleasure
The whole world must feel the glow

There's someone I love to entertain
So much more than any other
I know that you would never guess
He is my Latin Lover

Ode To Cynthia

Cynthia' has just had a birthday
And she's reached the big 60,
Of course you'd never guess it
She's such a slim young thing you know.

Now she's reached the magic number
there is no saying "no",
For now she has a bus pass
to take her where she wants to go

It is no problem now for her
to go on a shopping spree,
she has still a year or two to go though
Before she catches up with me.

And while her brand new bus pass
has filled her full of glee
I wonder if she's realised yet
That she can go and swim for free?

Perfect Prose

I've tried not once but many a time,
To write a poem that does not rhyme.
Yet something way down deep inside
Tells me, there is no reason without rhyme.
No matter how I've tried.

If rhyme is not the style you chose;
Then write a perfect piece of prose
Because if rhyming is the norm,
Without it there is neither shape nor form.

There are some wonderful forms of prose
That are as perfect as a full blown rose,
Sadly these are not for me
As I only write in rhyme you see.

The Single Life!

There is something about
Being on your own
Though it is not what should
Really be done.
There should be two.
Someone living with you
To stop you from looking so glum.

They say that romance is dead
And, it has to be said
That in some cases this may be true
But since I met you
I have never been blue
And I'm so glad that this one,
became two

The Phlebotomist

It's an ideal job for a VAMPIRE
At the ready for his blood collection
With needles, syringes and cotton wool
All there for that last minute injection

Each month I queue in the surgery
I don't ever give blood myself
Until the Phlebotomist takes it from me
And says it is good for my health

I don't fear the use of the needles
I am sure that blood tests are useful
But why must they be so greedy
And always take a whole armful?

Again we are back to the Vampire
At last his talent's unfurled
He takes blood from us all in the hospitals
and gets cash from the rest of the world

Valentine

Will you put your had in mine
Keep your slippers next to mine
And when we go to bed at night
Be the one who holds me tight

Will you repeat the words you say
Not just today but every day
Strolling softly in the dark
As we wander through the park

Will I always feel this way?
As we go on from day to day
Knowing that when I'm close to you
I can be sure you feel the same way too

Will you take me to the dance?
Every time you have the chance
Knowing that when I'm in your arms
I am captivated by your charms.

Will you say that you'll be mine
That you'll be my Valentine
Give me your love our whole life through
Just the way that I love you

The Romantic Writer

Roxy Monroe was a writer
The most romantic woman I know
Who was always looking for the chance
Her latest work to show
Her epic tales of love and romance
Were envied by many who longed for the chance
To find such a love in their own lives
And one day become husbands and wives
Roxy Monroe was the pseudonym
Of someone named Freddie Turner
A notorious man who committed a murder
When the new of this foul deed finally came out
The readers learned what it was all about
Freddie Turner was imprisoned for life
For the brutal murder of his wife

War and Peace

High hangs the dagger that drips with blood
People busy with talk about war
Never a thought for those without food
Gone are the days of Robin Hood.

Our country is in turmoil
It's Leaders have gone away
Never a thought for those in need
It's time for their holiday

The economy has gone downhill
The people struggle to pay their way
What are our leaders doing?
They're off on holiday

The dagger, it still hangs there
A constant bloody threat
But come on folks do not despair
We'll have a new government yet!

Now the blood from the dagger drips faster
When will we learn our fate
Will they take from the rich to give to the poor
Save our country before it's too late

The Caravan In Wartime

During the war we were evacuated
We lived in a caravan in Mablethorpe
It wasn't a proper caravan
It was a converted railway carriage
But we loved it
There were two family's living there
Every day we collected mushrooms
From the Farmers field
We could not go on to the beach
It was a minefield,we had fun just the same
We'd never been to the seaside before
So everything was a novelty
We were only there for one summer
When we came home that October
Our Mum gave birth to our brother
The family were overjoyed
Four years later the war had ended
There was peace at last

Our Friendly Ghost

Sometimes we find her in a corner
Playing with her toys.
She isn't very sociable
Not like other girls and boys.

She sits there by the cupboard
Where all the toys are kept,
Playing there quite calmly
One would think she never slept.

We don't know when she came here
This lovely little girl
She doesn't really belong to us
But now we've named her Pearl

She arrived here quite by accident
With a minimum of fuss.
And our Mum doesn't seem to mind
Her being here with us.

We cannot touch or hold her
To comfort her when she cries
This ghostly little figure
Who has such pain within her eyes

The Weather

What can be said about the weather?
Whether it rain or whether it snows
Something along these lines
is the way that it goes

Will it be a scorcher this summer?
Or even a showery spring
Perhaps we shall have a white Christmas
Who knows what the seasons will bring

Whenever we go on holiday
Whether by plane, by train, or by bus
A good way to start conversation begins
'Do you think the weather will be good to us'

Of one thing I am very sure
Whether there be rain or snow
You and I will always be
Together, forever

Happy Daze

Pitch patch pepper' oh happy days
The skipping rope and the school yards
And all those games that we played

Pitch patch pepper,
we need a skipping rope
Oh look here's Mummy's washing line
Just right for us I hope.

Oh look she's left a clothes peg
Fastened in the line
I wonder, had it begun to rain
As she took the washing from the line

Now at last our friend is here
We all call her Peppa pig
We always watched the programmes
But now I've grown too big

Those childhood days we've left behind,
Shall we forget them? Never
The Pepper, the Pig and the Clothes Peg,
We shall remember them forever

The Robot

Robert the robot
Is my very best friend
When anything is broken
He is the one who can mend

His mechanical mind
Is never stuck fast
He mends all in sequence
From the first to the last

He'd been out on a journey
from Mars to Venus
As he turned for home
He had not even seen us

Then he came down to earth
A t the very last minute
So fast in fact that his
Spacecraft smashed into it

Now he has no choice
But to stay here
And my message to him
Has always been clear

If you do all my jobs
And stay in a good mood
I'll make sure that you are
Fed and watered for good

Madness

I think I'm going out of my skull
In my life there is never a lull
I am so busy my head's in a tizzy
I must be out of my skull

I go out every day,the plan
Is work rest and play
It just doesn't work any more
Sometimes things get so bad
I can't figure it out
And fall asleep on the floor

When I sit down to write
It's the middle of the night
But somehow the words just won't come
What can I do? my time is so full
I'm sure I'm going out of my skull

Our Trip to the Sea

The sun is high in the sky
And the weather is warm,
The sea is perfectly calm.
Slowly it moves away from the shore
The tide is on the turn once more.
Today the sea is very blue
While the surf is pearly white
Summer has arrived at last
And the weather is put to rights
There are hot sunny days
And calm restful nights.
When we are on holiday
and the weather is good
We never make any plans
Just grab our swim suits and towels
And spend our time on the sands.
Our hotel is good and
they make lots of plans
To keep their guests happy
With bingo and dance
Then when it's all over
We shall fly back home
And wait for the next time
Our holidays come round

Clutter

"I'll never get rid of all this clutter"
The woman said with a mutter
The place looked as though a bomb had hit it
How she wished there was nothing in it

Piles of books collecting dust
"I'll have to get rid I really must"
Ornaments and magazines
Pictures showing Autumn scenes

Clothes I'll never wear again
The charity shops would really gain
Chance for them to earn some cash
Down to the shops I'll have to dash

Maybe tomorrow I'll begin
Oh no, working on Sunday's a mortal sin
Well, perhaps the beginning of next week
A couple of hours time I must seek

Six months later, just the same
Still lots of clutter, a different game
Now it's a brand new fashion range,
The sign of a woman who cannot change

Traffic

These days there always seems to be
Too much traffic on the road
It makes me glad to think that I
Am such a lucky toad

The neighbourhood in which I live
Is quite countrified,
And being a toad crossing such a busy road
Just leaves me terrified

The traffic always moves so fast
It just scares the life in me
And now I am old can't you see
How I worry how long I will last?

I am so determined to delay my fate
I hope you will all realise that
I shall try to make sure that my demise
Will arrive not sooner but late

I have so many things to do
I am sure you will all appreciate
That when I finally have to go
I shall be late when I reach Heavens Gate

There'll be lots of new things to look at
And the scenery will be just great
Above all a new understanding of death
Will make me much happier than of late

Now I'm travelling a different road
No longer am I a miserable toad
My whole existence is under my thumb
Since an Angel I've become.

There is an air of contentment
In this new place for me
A whole new way of living you see
And after all is said and done

There is an air of contentment
In this new place for me
A whole new way of living you see
And after all is said and done

There is an air of contentment
In this new place for me
A whole new way of living you see
And after all is said and done
It seems that I am still the lucky one

The Bed

I've had a really busy day
The woman said
Every single minute
has been spent in that bed

I've dug and I've hoed and weeded
Never even stopped for lunch
Spent all my time pulling up the weeds
Ending up with a great big bunch

At last the day is over
And all my work is done
The bulbs are in and the plants as well
As all the passers by will tell

Now I can relax and have a bath
Too much bending is no good for my head
no more walking up and down that path
I just can't wait to get into my bed

Transport

Like everyone in the world today
I use transport every day
It may not be the traditional kind
I can travel the world within my mind

I sit down after a hard days work
My imagination does not shirk
I am transported far and wide
To every corner of the countryside

Sometimes it's an island in the sun
Visited and loved by everyone
Some days I travel to the Heavens above
To be reunited with those that I love

Taken to the days that used to be
When you shared this earth with me
I am content, not often sad
And so thankful for all that I've had

I have my imagination to transport me
Any place in the universe I choose to be
This type of travel is for everyone,
Traffic jam free, and lots of fun

Holidays Past, Present and Future

Our Mother said to us one day
"We are going away to stay
In a place beside the sea
It cannot be called a holiday
Because our country is at war.
But we shall stay in a caravan
at a place close by the shore

We could not play upon the beach
And neither could we paddle
As far as donkeys were concerned
We never got near the saddle
And we kids could only dream
About the taste of vanilla ice cream

Many years passed by and then
I went to the seaside once again
By this time I had a husband
and children of my own
This holiday was quite recently
Another one chosen by the sea

Ice creams and fairgrounds
penny arcades the lot
Not one thing did we forget
The holiday was over before we knew it
But we enjoyed every single minute

The years they are passing
And the children are grown
they have left to live lives of their own
now we can learn to live life as we please.
Stay home and daydream or live life with ease

Now we look forward to our very next trip
we're going travel on a space ship
first to Venus and then on to Mars
then if there's time take a look at the stars

Another kind of Angel

When someone dies and goes to heaven
An Angel they become, or so I have been told.
What happens if you are sent to Hell
Do a Devil you become?
I wouldn't know for I have never seen one.
Whoever decides where we should go
Whether it be up or down
Maybe it was the way he lived his life
Or was he a bad man to his wife
And if you are sent to Heaven
Were you so perfect you were a pain
Or is there someone glad to be rid
Who puts you on that lofty plain
Many things about Angels
Have often been said
But whether they be black or white
They still are just as dead.

Ramblings of an old woman

I'm wandering through a field of slime
Remembering a much happier time
And looking forward to the day
When I shall travel far away

Now the siren roars along
With its unforgettable song.
An ambulance attending an accident
There goes another life that's spent

Now it's time to develop another song
And find a word that can't go wrong
Then perhaps somewhere sometime
I shall write a poem with rhyme.

In our house we have a new tenant
He floats around carrying a pennant
Just like the one in Wildfell hall
He is only another Ghost after all.

I think that I have just lost my bottle
I'm desperately looking for someone to throttle
Why did I ever go down this road?
Perhaps I shall find the slimy Toad

Writing in this way can be quite Chaotic
I think I could do with an antibiotic
I think I'll leave it 'til later my friend
Because at long last, I've reached the end

Boots

What is this obsession
we have with boots?
There are Wellington boots,
Riding boots, and football boots
Then there are even car boots
Where we can take them to
When we want rid of them
There are those we keep for
Skiing and for skating
And even those extra special ones
For when we go out dating
We keep our Wellington boots
To tackle the weather
And our hiking boots
to walk through the heather.
I have often wondered though
And the thought is not very nice.
Why do we never think of using our skates
When we are walking on thin ice?

When

When I was young I had lots of ideas
When I was young I used to say my prayers.
When I was young I wanted to sail on the seas.
When I was young I was taught to say please

When I was young I wanted to sing
When I was young I wanted to try everything
When I was married our children were born.
When we were older our marriage was torn

The years have passed and our children have flown
Out into the world to live lives of their own
Whilst I, alas am Left all alone

Films

There are many, many films
That I have been to see.
And I reckon there are many others,
Who would like to watch with me?

I have laughed with Mother Riley
And our oldest friend Popeye
Yet there were many other films
That always made me cry.

Films like Phantom of the Opera
And the famous Wuthering Heights.
Not forgetting Samson and Delilah,
Who gave me lots of sleepless nights

Going My Way, Was winner in its day?
It always made me want to sing
And there was no better way to do it
than with our old friend Bing

Mary Poppins, and Singin' in the Rain
were always very popular
We saw them time and time again
And should we ever get the chance
We'd watch them all again

Friend of a Friend

I know a friend of a friend of mine
Who enjoyed drinking lots of wine
He used to be quite a clever man
Until he drank anything
that came out of a can

In time his job began to suffer
Of that there is no doubt
All one can say about him
He is just a lazy lout

one day I met this friend of mine
She was all bruised and sore
Needless to say this boozy man
Is her friend no more

Gloves

What has happened to the days
When the ladies all wore gloves
The times when we were dressed to kill
we always wore our gloves at will

When it came to evening dress
Our ball gowns were the very best
Gloves were worn up to the elbows
In the style that everyone knows

On formal and family occasions
At weddings and the like
If you were seen without hat and gloves
Then be prepared to take a hike

Dressing up and going to town
Is something that the ladies all love
But how many are there nowadays
Who go out wearing gloves

If A Plumber Cannot Do It

When you have a tap that leaks
Central heating that bubbles and squeaks
Or a washing machine that grunts and groans
You need a handy man

Kitchens and bathrooms are high on his list
Something so vital would be sadly missed
A plumber is a very clever man
If he cannot do the job then no one can.

Whenever I go to bed at night
As soon as I turn out the light
And jump into bed with my husband Dan
I'm very sure that if anyone can do it
I know a man who can

My Special Child

His eyes flutter and I shake
His hands tremble and I hold my breath
I want to take him in my arms
This child I love so much
Of all my boys he is the one
Who needs such special care
He needs to know that night and day
We shall be there for him if he should call
We shall be there to hold him
if he should fall

Mothering Sunday

Today I spent time in the garden
Watching the young folks pass by
They had smiles on their faces
And carried flowers, bottles and cards

For this a special day is for Mothers
The person we love more than life
Someone who is always there for us
not just when there's trouble and strife

My Mum is no longer with us
but now I'm a mum myself
and I know that whatever becomes
me, I shall never be left on the shelf

Magazines

I've been searching through my dictionary
And even on my PC
To learn something about magazines
and how elusive they can be.

Then suddenly there they were
out on the internet
Woman's Weekly, Woman's own
and lots of girlie stuff

There wasn't very much for men
On this site I'd found
But wait a minute what have we here
P C Pro, What Car? and Top Gear

Not to mention Gardeners World
Health and Fitness, FHM and Zoo,
also one Arena Homme
That's a new one on me too

But after all is said and done
they are only sheets of news
Surely there's some other way
to chase away the blues

If we keep looking long enough
We shall find the answers that we crave
And if that becomes a problem
We can always flirt with Dave

My Bicycle

My very first wheels were bought for me
When I was only three
Mummy and Daddy bought a trike for me
No cycling then for a long, long time
Twelve years past before the very next spree
By that time I was going to work you see.

There wasn't much cash in those far off days
"You'll have to save up for a bit" my Father says
For a while there can be no bike
So for the time being you'll just have to hike."

Then one day right out of the blue
Our Mum says
"come here lass I'd like a word with you"
I stood there wondering if I'd done anything wrong
"How would you like a bicycle all your own?

Not new its true, but to you t' would belong?
I know someone who has a bicycle just for you
But it might take some time to get it to you
Your cousin Edna has outgrown her own
And is getting a new one very soon

When I was asked if I knew anyone who
could make use of an old bike I thought about you
It would mean that you won't have to hike any more.
You can cycle to work from door to door."

Edna didn't want you to be feeling blue
Aunt Minnie will put it on the train just for you
The next train from Manchester she said it would be
We can pick it up from the station at half past three.

My English Teacher

I had an English Teacher
Who I liked very much.
She was very, very special
And we always kept in touch.

The best thing that she gave to me
Was a lasting love of poetry
She taught me how to write in rhyme
And always seemed to have the time

Some of the poems that she taught me
I can remember them by heart
And even when I write today
She always plays a part.

And if the children misbehaved
She knew just how to stop them
A very strict no nonsense type
Our very dear Miss Topsham

Murder in my mind

Almost every day I wake up
With murder in my mind
He's really not a bad man
And I feel so unkind

He is a man that I know well
He's driving me insane
Usually we get on very well
But he can be such a pain

No matter what the subject
He is always in the right
And even when he isn't
There has to be a fight

I get so angry I could kill him
My life is such a bind
It shouldn't be too difficult
When I have murder in my mind

Revenge

Why do we always think
When one does wrong
That we must have revenge
Why can't we take another way
And try to right that wrong?
When will enemies ever learn
That when both sides are unforgiving
There never will be any peace
And life not worth the living

Rising Damp

The garden was damp with
summer rain
The flowers were lifting
their heads again
As we walked along
the country road
We were overtaken
by a very large toad
He had obviously enjoyed
The falling rain and now he is
On his way home again

Remembrance

Two Veterans in the Andale centre
Beside a visitors stand
Bringing poppies to the people
Armistice day is at hand

They fought with our lads
In the Second World War
And remember all those
Who died, in the wars before

The one thing that unites us all
Is the sight of those poppies
As there wearers stand tall
At the cenotaph of remembrance
Now they stand there side by side
Remembering sadly all those who died
A simple prayer that this fighting will cease
That together we might learn to live in peace.

The poppies that grew in Flanders field
Not only the bloodshed did they reveal
But the hope for the future that the lads fought for
And their wish for an end to this bloody war

Sleepless in Cross gates

When I go to bed each night
And close my bedroom door
I can't suppress the hatred
That I've felt so many times before

The nights have robbed me of my sleep,
Hours and hours of counting sheep.
And aeroplanes that cross the skies,
Yet precious sleep evades my eyes.

I walk the floor while others slumber
Finally into bed I clamber
Sleepless still, I find I'm shaking
As once again, the dawn is breaking.

Sunshine

Everyone loves the sunshine
It keeps our spirits high
As welcome as a glass of wine
Though I often wonder why

Each time we go on holiday
We always chase the sun
Hoping that every single day
Will be just right for everyone

Whenever we go on holiday
We forget our pains and ills
Sometimes if we're lucky
We don't even need our pills

We visited a Cathedral
Just the other day
And as we walked out of the door
The sun came out to play

There always is a day or two
When there is a shower
Then we have to stay indoors
If only for an hour

Suddenly the sun comes out again
And we forget about the rain
And wander down to the waterside
Just to sunbathe and watch the tide

Now our holiday is over
We leave to catch the train
Or some other form of transport
That will take us home again

The Pawnbroker

Long ago when times were hard
And I were nobbut a lass
The ordinary working folk
Never had a lot o' brass

Seven days a week they worked
for nowt more than a pittance,
And much of their pride
was not hard to hide
All those years ago

Their earnings were never big enough
To feed and clothe their families and such
Mum would attack the fire with a poker
When considering the options of the Pawnbroker

There was no plastic or ATM
To help them raise the cash back then
While going to a pawnbroker
Was considered very rash

Every Tuesday our Mum would pop
Down to Uncles the local pawn shop
Back home there was no need for the door to lock
'Cos owt that was worth owt was going into hock

Dad's best suit, Mum's Sunday coat
And all our Whitsie clothes were sent
To raise the money to pay the rent
All she got was seven and a tanner
Not even enough to raise a banner

On a Wednesday Mum paid the rent
With the seven and a tanner that she'd
Got out of Uncle at the pawn shop
But it would take eight and a tanner
to get the stuff back before it went under the hammer

When Friday came and Dad had been paid
Being the eldest, I was sent with the
Pawnbrokers ticket and the Eight and six
To reclaim the stuff that got us out of a fix

Later that night as Dad turned out the light
He could hear Mum as her prayers she said
And when at last he climbed into bed
He too thanked God for the roof over our heads

The Great Yorkshire Show

I've never been to the Yorkshire Show
It's not a place I ever wanted to go
But when we were asked to write about it today
I hadn't a clue what I was going to say

I went home and did some research that night
To see what went on and find out if I might
Be interested in going along to see
All the exciting things there are going to be.

Apart from the agricultural shows
The cattle the pigs and the sheep
You can spend all day, stroll round with ease.
You can surely find something there
that will please

There's motor cross and falconry
A cheese and dairy show
There are even show jumpers
Who are prepared to take a bow

So tonight I'm going on the net
To view, and book my ticket
With all the things that are going on
There might even be game of cricket

The Trip

Now is the time for me
To take a trip to the stars,
Maybe up to Venus
Or even on to Mars.

Where to go or what to do
My thoughts are so divided.
Somehow I can't make up my mind
Why am I undecided?

Perhaps I could take myself
to America, and
spend some time befriending
A different type of star?

Or maybe I should fly away
To Paris, or even Rome
And never give another thought
To ever coming home.

Decision made I know at last,
Where I want to be
I'm going to take a trip down South,
And visit my family

The Hedgehog

There's a hedgehog in my garden
He's been there for many a day
I'm always there to se him
When he comes around to play

He's nobbut just a baby
You only have to look
But one day when he is full grown
Perhaps I'll write a book

I'm so happy that he chose me
To come and share my life
And now that he is older
I can't wait to meet his wife

Soon when there are children
Born to this lovely pair
I shall give them lots of food
for all of them to share

The Instrumentalist

One of my Grandsons'
Is a musician, an Instrumentalist,
If you were to ask him what he plays
Then he has quite a list

Up among his favourites
Are the tenor and baritone sax
If he gets the chance to play at all
We never have to ask

He also plays acoustic guitar
And clarinet as well
He loves his music very much
As anyone an tell

He used to be a member
Of a very good rock band
It was called 'The Reborn Flames'
I don't remember all their names
It was some time ago

Their education won the day and
The band has been laid to rest
Though not to be abandoned
With time it will stand the test

With hard work and determination
They will be up there with the best
I'm sure they'll play again some day
But only time, will be the test

The Grand Theatre

Last night we went to the theatre
To a drama being shown at the Grand
It was the premier of Jekyll and Hyde
The curtain had scarcely arisen
When we were all ushered outside

The fire bell had started a ringing
Though no one could quite understand
Why the stage filled with smoke
But it was no joke!
Suddenly everything got out of hand

The show was almost a sell out
Nearly all the tickets were sold
Fire engines were swiftly arriving
While we stood around in the cold

First one,then two and finally three
but alas there was very little to see.
onlookers were gathering around us
They couldn't understand all the fuss

A fireman appeared on the doorstep,
his helmet held under his arm
Wiping the sweat from his forehead
He said there is no cause for alarm

After a while we were ushered inside
For truly the show must go on.
to our surprise the curtain started to rise
we were ready for the play to go on

Three Score Years And Ten

Dear Friend, This is the time of year,
When you're reminded that
Your birthdays near.
the time is coming round again
this time,it's three score years and ten.

Time to reflect upon your life,
When you were Schoolgirl,
teenager, mother, wife,
Did your life turn out the way
you planned,
Or was it changed by a Mightier hand?

Did your wildest dreams come true?
When decisions that were made
Were up to you.
Did you always follow the sensible way?
Or throw caution to the wind
And live just for the day?

Now your seventieth birthdays here,
It's the start of another exciting year,
You may find it hard to travel, and yet
The world is your oyster, out on the Internet.

The Postcard

Whenever they go on holiday
My family always send me a card
Whether it's from Portugal Greece or Rome
They always send a card back home

My daughter always tells me how
their journey happens to be
A s soon as their plane touches down
She finds the time to write to me

There is always a comment on
Their hotel, the pool and the food
These three things are important
To ensure that their holiday is good

Next there comes a line about
what sightseeing they have done
And an epistle always comes
when they are having fun

One thing I always ask myself
At night when I'm alone
why does the damn thing always arrive
Two weeks after they've come back home?

The Single Life!

There is something about
Being on your own
Though it is not what should
Really be done.

There should be two.
Someone living with you
To stop you from looking so glum.

They say that romance is dead
And, it has to be said
That in some cases this may be true
But since I met you

I have never been blue
And I'm so glad that this one,
I have never been blue
And I'm so glad that this one,
became two

Victoria Blake

There once was a very beautiful girl
Her name was Victoria Blake
Loved and admired by those handsome men
Who travelled miles for her sake

Everyone knew she had a passion you see
And they all longed to take her out to tea
For Miss Victoria Blake had a passion for cake
The type that her Mother used to bake

The lightest sponge, lighter than an Angels breath
Filled with strawberry jam and cream
They are the kind of cakes that are everyone bakes
The ones that are every cooks dream

She never said no to the chance to go out
And have strawberry cakes for tea
But after a while, though she ate with style
The cake stuck to her hips you see.

She and the cakes were so popular
It was not long before the two became one
Which is why whenever we buy,
We ask for two Victoria sponges, not one

What If

What if the family are too hard up
To pay for an old mans funeral car
And they carried the coffin on to the bus
where all the passengers are

If the bus dropped them off
at the cemetery gate,
strapped for time and couldn't wait
What then would be the old man's fate

If the family carried a coffin
That was much too heavy and more
Then in no time at all that same coffin
Would have fallen to the floor

Then suddenly the lid flew off
Revealing the body of that same little Toff
Who stirred, rubbed his eyes
And looked up at the skies shouting
"In God's name where the hell am I?

Written wiv a Stick

When I was a child I used to write
In the sand wiv a stick
Everyone said that I must have been thick
But I'll fool them all before I'm done
Cos' I'm back in school 'til I'm twenty one

As I grew older I became Much, much bolder
I was old enough To run off with a soldier
When I come back home I shall make them all see
That I'm not so thick As everyone thought me to be

Things never change In just a tick
And everyone thinks That I'm still a bit thick
Next week I shall invite them to the University
Where they can come And watch me
Pick up my very first English degree

Water

Can you imagine life without any H 2 0?
A life not worth the living no place for us to go.
If there were no water for our Ale, Coffee or Tea
It would be a very sad life for You and Me

There'd be no way to clean our crocks
Or even wash our sweaty socks
There'd be no ice to ski or skate
No pools to swim in at a later date

Whenever it begins to rain
we don our hats and mac's again
Never do we forget our brolly's
In our dash to the supermarket
Where we grab our trolleys

Glad to be indoors again
Shielded from the wind and rain
Without the it we would not have
Any vegetables, fruit or flowers
No gardens for us to while away the hours

When everything is said and done
To have no water wouldn't be much fun,
it is taken for granted you must agree.
But we shall none of us miss it
'til it affects you and me

Cleaning

It is time to get your act together
And get some cleaning done
Clear out those dated memories
Go out and have some fun

Life's too short to sit around
Spending your time alone
You must clean up those memories
The one's you treasure most
And lock them safely in your heart
To make sure they'll never be lost

It is time for you to go out now
And begin a brand new life
It doesn't matter what you do
Don't spend your time alone
Just go out and have some fun
Remember you're the lucky one!

Notepad

I've been looking for my note pad,
Searching everywhere.
On the table, on the floor
And even under my chair.

I've no idea what's happened to it
Will someone tell me what to do,
If it doesn't turn up soon
I don't know what I'll do

I write down all my things 'To do'
I have to use it every day
Just to keep my sanity
Before I put it away

I even write my shopping list
Before going to the store
And go out and leave it on the table
Need I say any more?

The next place I am going to look
will be on my computer
I've seen an icon on the screen
Maybe it's got in through the router

That could make life a little difficult
If I have to write it down on screen
Going shopping with a computer
I would feel such a jerk

Just before you interrupt
And say why not use your printer
Let me tell you only once
The damn thing doesn't work

Directions

Just turn right at the racecourse
She said with a smile
Keep straight on for about a mile
Pass the great barn and the flower show
The next turn left is the way to go
When you turn the next corner
the airports in sight and
you'll make the journey
in good time for your flight

Through the Window

People are dancing in the hall,
Everyone is having a ball.
Through the window I see them there
Dressed in posh clothes, with pristine hair.
Outside where I stand it's a different tale,
Some of these men are just out of jail.
Standing by, waiting for some work to do,
One man stands there holding a shoe.
That was all that he had in the slammer,
A shoe to beat the nails in with.
It was not an option, there was no hammer.

Mice

Mice are tiny little beings
That are no strangers to me
Each time I went into the mill
There were always plenty to see

They would climb into the baskets
Where the weavers kept their bobbins
And many a time you would hear a shout
If a mouse climbed someone's stockings

All around the weaving sheds
Were holes along the walls
where each mouse had built it's home
Only going back there
When they were too tired to roam

And once, one long hot summer
Scurrying down the mill yard
They all turned out en masse
No room for anyone to pass

When they reached the bottom
On the edge of the canal side
They dashed ahead with a great big rush
And jumped in at the waterside

My Cat

I dearly love the old black cat
my Gran bestowed on me
She said he'd be my guardian
and my guide, be forever by my side.

And though I've never see him
I know he's always there,
The way he rubs around my legs
when I sit in my chair.

When I sit down to watch TV,
I feel him climb upon my knee
Knowing I don't like being alone,
he snuggles down in his comfort zone

There are days when I forget
about him always being there,
I have to stop and say a quick prayer,
when I stumble and trip over him

To me he will always be
Warm, faithful, loving
and things like that,
Bu t he'll always be there
my silly old cat

Our Budgie

We have a little budgie
With feathers that are blue,
Such a gorgeous little bird,
Just right for me and you

He sits there happily on his perch
A chattering all day long
The minute you get home from work
The chat becomes a song

You must be sure to speak to him
As soon as you get in,
Or he will screech and shout,
And scatter his seed about
Until your patience wears thin.

To flutter to your shoulder and rub
His head against your cheek
For a gentle and more loving pet
You don't have far to seek

A Grand Cup of Tea

Today I went into the city
To go on a shopping spree.
All went well and I bought
lots of things. It's just amazing
what a good day brings

I enjoy my walks around the town
But now and again I have to sit down
So I went to the café for a cup of tea
And to my surprise a celebrity came
And sat himself right next to me.

We sat and we chatted and acted the clown
Until at last the sun went down
And when I disclose who it was
It will bring down the house
Because my new mate
Is our friend Mickey Mouse

Adam and Sarah

Very soon there's going to be
A wedding in our family
Our eldest Grandson it will be
And we shall welcome Sarah to the family

The years have flown since he was born
Now he has grown up and gone
out into the world to make a life of his own
Madly in love with the lovely Sarah

They are so very happy together
This is a love that will last forever
We his family miss him very much
But they will always keep in touch

He and Sarah visit us quite a lot
Using up any spare time they have got
I can't wait to see them as they walk down the aisle
The day that will make the whole family smile

We shall look forward to the day when we shall see
That happy day when those two become three

A Letter to
A New Friend

Dear Anne I think we've started
Something very new.
The beginnings of a friendship
In a banking queue.

We struck up a conversation
Whilst waiting for our chance
To get our business over
Without too much hindrance

We are very busy people
And standing in a queue
Is not for folks like Ann and I
Who have lots of things to do

When finally we got out of there
We headed off to "Flavours"
Which is the local coffee shop
That everybody favours

We sat there with our coffee
And talked for hours on end
But by the time we left there
We each had found a new friend.

A Dainty Little Box

It was nobbut just a little box
Hexagonal in shape
Coloured pink and blue and lilac
With a bow of silk yellow tape

It looks just like a girlie box
That's been around a year or two
You can tell that by the knocks
It's much too small to house party frocks

If someone handed it to you
I wonder just what you would do?
maybe someone has something to hide
Should we take to take a look inside

Maybe some amorous lover
who can't wait to hand it over
A diamond ring for the girl of his dreams
A fancy box is not always what it seems

Autumn

The season is back with us once more
Colours mellowed as before
One last burst of ripening beauty
Once again nature has done her duty
Taking care of the flowers and trees

Wafting them gently in the autumn breeze
Making them ready for their winter sleep
All the while her vigil she will keep
Until Jack Frost appears once more
The herald of winter arrives as before

An easy Exercise Guide

When Jayne was but a teenager
She set herself a guide
An easy exercise on what to do
Once she became a bride.

She devised a very clever way
Of how to wash and iron
And once that exercise was done
She taught herself another one

She decided that the way to go
Was how to feed her Man
So the cooking and the baking
Was the next part of her plan

Next came the DIY and decorating
Not a bad thing for a lady in waiting
Making beds and cleaning floors
Soon she was proficient at all her chores

From there she went to entertaining,
How to dress and how to behave
And how to work without complaining
One thing that she didn't crave
was how to be a young mans slave
Next came the happiest day of her life
The day that she and Johnny wed
The easiest exercise of her life
Was learning how to be a good wife

The Script Writer

I have been asked to write a comedy script
About comedians from the past
Between Arthur Askey and Benny Hill
Something humorous at last.

Arthur and Benny were comedians
In their own write
Very, very funny and also very bright
If I should get the whole thing wrong
I wouldn't want to cause a fright

Comedy writing is just not my style
Doug and Vic can do better by far
When the curtain goes up and the applause begins
We know how good our scriptwriters are

The Mirror

A mirror or a looking glass
Is a good friend to many a lass
Especially just before a date
She must look just right and not be late

Maybe they'll go out to a dance
If they ever get the chance
For that she'll need to look just right
Can't give folks a fright when it gets to midnight

After a while going out with this Guy
They may even get a chance to fly
Off they'll go to foreign climes
And have a really wonderful time

Perhaps one day this lover and his lass
Might even wed, it could come to pass
And all because this looking glass
Was the pride and joy of a lovely Lass

Blackpool in Winter

The sea is harsh yet happy
The world is cold as ice
When winter comes
It certainly takes
Blackpool in it's vice

The visitors walk along the prom
In scarves and hats galore
They must have fallen for the place
They have all been here before

Breaking up

When there Is a break up within a family,
It always causes heartache
for those who mean the world you see
It is not only with those who are
breaking up where the heartache lies

It is with the Mum's and Dads
and Grandma's who lie awake and cry
The tears are for the little ones
Deprived of Mum or Dad
While Grandmas just compare it
With those precious times they've had

There would be no unwanted children
and marriages that never last
They would be for a lifetime
And forever they would last
The children would have two parents
A Mother and a Dad
And grow up with security and love
Just the way we had

Carole and Little Mikey

Hello Carole
Will you come and play with me
Come here Carole
In your carriage and talk to me.

I can't come and play today
I'm out with Grandpa Mike
He says if I'm a good boy
I can take my trike,

Carole you know that Granpa
Is your neighbour,
and he is called Big Mike,
but it is only Little Mikey
Who gets to ride the trike.

Maybe if I asked him
You could bring your carriage
It could be real handy
To carry all the baggage

Better go now Carol I can see
Your Dad is looking for you
Maybe when the shopping's done
We could have some tea

God Bless little Mikey
He is only three

Easter Time

At last the spring is here once more,
and Easter is upon us.
The daffodils are coming out
and rabbits start a playing

Trees and flowers begin to grow,
and before too long
The world will know
it's Eastertide once more

The clocks have changed and days grow long
And the birds are bursting into song
The children play and dance with glee
Around the Maypole for all to see

With winter far behind us
And good weather still to come
There will be lots of gardening
And picnics going on

Then all too soon school holidays are here
The children are so delighted
No more school for six whole weeks
But Mums aren't too excited

Before too long the summers gone
The nights are getting longer
There's bonfire chumping to be done
And fireworks to buy

Now Christmas is upon us
and it's wintertime once more
with snowmen and roasted chestnuts
And presents by the score

And then before we know it
Before we know quite where we are
The trees and flowers show us
That it's Easter time once more

Sands of Time

A clock is like the sands of time
Ticking our lives away
It is always there whatever we do
At work, at rest or play.

Begins to tick at the time of our birth
And carries on as we travel the earth
Journeying along the paths of life
As Infant, Toddler, Teenager and Wife

Then when at last our journey is done
And we travel our lonely way
The clock of time ticks on and on
For a new life just begun

The Locket

Accept this little gift of mine
A souvenir of my love for you
A precious gift to help you through
As you walk the paths of life

Whether you are here at home
Or very far away
Remember that my love for you
Is with you all the way

Please accept this locket
It holds my heart and all my love
And know that every time you touch it
I shall be watching from above

Spawning Snow

Winter roared into the world engulfing it
with frost filled clouds, spawning snow.
Dawn breaks with a gentle rose pink glow.
Softly now like blossoms in a flower show,
nudging gently flakes of white into
the silence of the wintry night.

The snow so vast yet light, falls gently
to the earth in the silence of the night.
Next morning children stand in awe
of a pure white world they never saw before
A magic land, a wonderland.
I guess it must be Christmastime once more

Sunshine

Everyone loves the sunshine
It keeps our spirits high
As welcome as a glass of wine
Though I often wonder why

Each time we go on holiday
We always chase the sun
Hoping that every single day
Will be just right for everyone

Whenever we go on holiday
We forget our pains and ills
Sometimes if we're lucky
We don't even need our pills

We visited a Cathedral
Just the other day
And as we walked out of the door
The sun came out to play

There always is a day or two
When there is a shower
Then we have to stay indoors
If only for an hour

Suddenly the sun comes out again
And we forget about the rain
And wander down to the waterside
Just to sunbathe and watch the tide

Now our holiday is over
We leave to catch the train
Or some other form of transport
That will take us home again

The Maid Saw It All

The Lord of the Manor is a handsome man
Who chats up the ladies whenever he can.
Somebody had said he was riding for a fall
And I have no doubt, that the Maid saw it all.

It makes no difference that he is a married man
He still chats up the ladies whenever he can
One night he fondled a Lass in the Hall
I expect you'll have guessed, the maid saw it all

Not getting caught was a large part of the fun
And there was no stopping this Lordly one,
Until he was caught in the bedroom and not in the hall
By the Maid, who at last had seen it all.

If I Ruled The World

It is easy to find solutions
When the responsibility is not mine
To have the authority to change
the world at any time

It is so easy to make changes
While sitting in the armchair
The boot is on the other foot
When there's no one there to care.

There would be no more
Unemployment and no more wars
No waiting lists and no more pain
All hospital patients would be well again

The young folks would go out to work
to provide pensions for all those
Who didn't shirk, and have
Laboured for the last forty five years

The best thing of all if I ruled the world
Everyone would be equal and live in harmony
Peace, love and tranquility there would be
For everyone, not just you and me

This Crazy World

The room was suddenly rich, and the great bay window
was infused with the warm red glow of the sunset
our summer had been long and hot, very hot
and now the last vestiges of its existence
were portrayed here for all to see

The whole house came alive with the warmth of it's glow
the whole world is crazier than we think
and yet we take her gifts for granted.
Abuse her generosity and love her seasons.

Sun has set and it is dusk already,
the first of autumn's leaves are falling
and rustling in the breeze,
the first signs of winter are beginning to appear

The whole world has turned on her head
and on the other side of the world
the summer is just beginning to appear.
Crazy, crazy world where is our place in the universe?

The Journey

As we journey through life there are such wonderful things
Like the glorious sunshine that a new day brings
Along with the cooing of doves as they flap their wings.
Or that heavenly look on a little child's face
And the rush of a waterfall in some quiet place
The sound of the rain on our window pane
Or the sight of the rainbow when it appears again.
All these things are a part of our life
On our journey each day as a child, husband or wife
We learn to appreciate the things that we love
Those Heaven sent gifts that come down from above

For Mary

My heart goes out to you
in your confusion and your fears
It aches for you in your
loneliness and tears

I feel the pain and the frustration
in your conviction of the things
That you have not done
That are not yet real

I worry that you may come to harm
Whilst you still live alone
And fear that one day soon
you may have to leave your home

Most of all I fear
That as you near the end
You will no longer recognise me
As your friend

A Tanner